OVERCOMING FEAR OF FAILURE

HONOR HEAD

W

FRANKLIN WATTS
LONDON • SYDNEY

Franklin Watts
First published in Great Britain in 2017 by The Watts Publishing Group

Credits:
Series Editor: Jean Coppendale
Series Designers: Steve Evans, Lorraine Inglis

Picture credits:
Every attempt has been made to clear copyright. Should there be any inadvertent omission please apply to the
publisher for rectification.
t = top, b = bottom , l = left, r = right, m = middle
Illustrations: pgs 6, 8, 26, Steve Evans Illustration
Backgrounds: pgs 12-13, 14-15, 18-19, vecteezy.com
Cover: © Shutterstock/MSSA
All images listed here are © of Shutterstock and: 4 dog, Javier Brosch; b, Incomible/5 Talkback heads
throughout, Dream Master/7 words, blue67design; thumbs up, Jane Kelly; frame, appler/10 background,
mbolina/12 background, Bloomicon/13 Churchill, Olga Popova/14 silhouette, Mindmo; b bun, pa3x/
16 cat-dog, Eric Isselee/17b left head, Beatriz Gascon J; Muhammad Ali, Tinseltown/19t, FotoYakov/20b,
itana/21t, anintov/ 22 lightbulb, jesadaphom; background ALMAGAMI; l, Helga Esteb; r, Mitch Gunn/
23t, Paolo Bona; mr, landmarkmedia; ml, Lodimup, br, Gong To/24 background, Boguslaw Mazur/
25r, JStone/26 background, Olga Milagros; Dalmatian, Eric Isselee/27t, lev radin/28 background, kampolz;
birds, Mrs. Opossum.

Note to parents and teachers: Every effort has been made by the Publishers to ensure that these websites are
suitable for children, that they are of the highest educational value, and that they contain no inappropriate or
offensive material. However, because of the nature of the Internet, it is impossible to guarantee that the contents
of these sites will not be altered. We strongly advise that Internet access is supervised by a responsible adult.

ISBN 978 1 4451 5288 2
Printed in China

Franklin Watts
An imprint of
Hachette Children's Group
Part of The Watts Publishing Group
Carmelite House
50 Victoria Embankment
London EC4Y 0DZ

An Hachette UK Company
www.hachette.co.uk

www.franklinwatts.co.uk

Contents

What is a fear of failure? 4

No one is born with a fear of failure........................... 6

Making mistakes 8

Do you have a fear of failure? 10

High expectations... 12

School stress.. 14

Friends for ever?... 16

Self-esteem and failure.. 18

Make failure a success... 20

Be inspired 22

What is *your* success?.. 24

Overcoming your fear 26

So, to recap 28

Glossary.. 30

Further information 31

Index.. 32

WHAT IS A FEAR OF FAILURE?

Fear of failure is feeling anxious about not getting good marks for a school project, feeling that you may not come first in a test or that you're not good enough to try out for a sports team without even bothering to try.

You're not alone

Lots of people suffer from a fear of failure. It's one of the biggest causes of anxiety and stress for school students. It's a fear that can affect people in many different ways. For some people, it can make them afraid to try new things. For others it means that they have to come first in everything they do.

For many a fear of failure is linked to low self-esteem. It can make people feel that they're not good enough at anything and it can ruin their self-confidence. Just as a fear of failure affects us in different ways, so we have different ways of coping with it.

Must be no.1

Some people have to be perfect at everything they do – failure is not an option. For these people failing at something means they are a failure as a person. They are so scared of failing that they spend much longer on, say, their homework, than the average student. Or if they feel they can't be top of the class, they don't bother to try at all.

They stick to activities they know they can do really well rather than trying new activities that they may not be so good at even though they might really enjoy them. This limits their choices and means they may not fulfil their full potential.

Can't be bothered!

Some people believe that if they try hard at something and then fail, it means they're really stupid. So for them the best option is not to really try at anything. Then they tell themselves that they failed not because they couldn't do it, but because they didn't try very hard. Sadly, by not trying hard enough they will never know whether they might have succeeded or not.

Students who just accept failure don't even bother to try. Maybe they've failed a lot in the past and their sense of self-worth is so low they don't think they will ever be able to do anything well no matter how hard they try. If they're successful at anything, they may believe the teacher gave them an easy task to do or it was a fluke that they did so well.

All this *stress* over failing! But failure can be the best thing that ever happened to you. Failure can lead to **success**.

TALKBACK!

Look out for the TALKBACK boxes. This is where you and your friends, family or classmates can discuss two sides of an argument. There are no right or wrong answers, but you might be surprised at the conclusions you come to.

SUCCESS

No one is born with a fear of failure

Our fear of failing or fear of getting things wrong develops as we get older. There are lots of reasons why this can happen.

Critical adults

Many people only give praise for good results, rather than praising the effort we make. Instead of telling us that we've done a great job for trying, they are critical when we get things wrong or because we didn't do well enough. The adults don't mean to hurt us or make us feel bad – mostly they only want what is best for us. But their criticism can seem unfair and can make us feel that we've let people down.

Feeling bad

Lots of people feel embarrassed and stupid when they get things wrong. They think people are laughing at them and judging them. Failing at something we really want to get right can also make us feel sad and disappointed. These negative feelings might put us off trying new things. After all, who wants to feel stupid, disappointed or embarrassed? But failing doesn't have to be like that. Successful people fail as much as anyone, but they learn to keep their failure in perspective. This means that although no one likes to fail, they don't see failure as defeat and give up, but see it as an opportunity to have another go.

Getting things **wrong** is part of everyday life. Everyone does it.

A-list lives

Everyday we are swamped with images and stories about well-known people – celebrities, sporting personalities and vloggers who are good looking, rich and successful. This makes some people feel that if they don't achieve great things and look fabulous all the time they have failed.

But the glamorous lifestyle is just what we see on the media and most celebrities work hard behind the scenes to achieve their success. And why strive to be like someone else? Work on your own unique strengths and be yourself.

PERFECT

100%

TALKBACK!

Here are two ways of looking at failing. Which one do you think is right and why?

If you keep on failing, you might as well give up. No point in trying.

If you keep on failing, you'll learn from your mistakes and you might succeed next time – it's got to be worth another try.

7

MAKING MISTAKES

We will all make mistakes, there's no way around that, so we have to get used to it. But instead of feeling bad when you do, think how you can make the mistake work for you.

Making an effort counts

Teachers or the people who look after us and care about us can get angry or upset when we make mistakes. They tell us off or say they are disappointed in us. This makes us feel bad so we don't try to do anything different or new in case we get it wrong and upset the adults again.

What we all have to remember (and this includes adults) is that it's trying your best to do something that is important, not whether you get it right or not. It's great when you do succeed, but getting it wrong is not bad. We have to learn to be proud of ourselves for making an effort and accept our mistakes.

Here to help

Ever wished you could hide a mistake under the carpet or just magic it away without anyone knowing? Everyone has. But discussing your mistakes with your teachers, family or even friends means other people can start to help you so you can get it right next time.

If you've given something your best shot and tried really hard, you shouldn't be embarrassed or ashamed if you get it wrong. Ask for help and try again.

Oops!

Mistakes are good

Making mistakes can be a good thing if we learn from them, whether it's to do with school work, friendships or hobbies. Here's how…

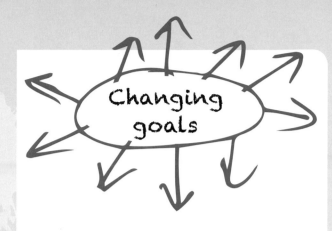

Changing goals

Making mistakes helps us learn to cope with failure and to move on. Sometimes we have to accept we can't do something no matter how hard we try.

When this happens we must try not get angry or upset. This can be hard but it helps us to learn about our strengths and weaknesses.

Everyone should have goals and dreams about what they want to achieve, but we don't always achieve our goals. That's okay – if something really isn't working, or you try your very best and can't get it right, maybe it's just not for you. Think about new goals. Being able to adapt your ideas to your strengths is a sign of growing up and taking control of your life.

Making mistakes can teach us how to deal with people. Perhaps you said or did something that really upset a friend, or made someone you care about angry. Now you know to be careful not to say or do that again, or to do it differently so it doesn't upset anyone.

Do you have a fear of failure?

Most people just move on if they get something wrong, or try again. Others find it much harder to deal with.

Comfort-zone prison

We all have a comfort zone. This is a place where we feel safe, secure and in control. Leaving our comfort zone can be like walking a tightrope without a safety net – really scary! Comfort zones are okay, but we need to get out of them sometimes in order to realise our full potential. People who fear failure often lack self-confidence and so don't feel strong enough to try anything new, so they always play it safe. They're nervous about learning new things, such as a new sport or a musical instrument, and don't try to make new friends in case they are rejected.

Making excuses

When people are scared of getting things wrong they make excuses for not doing something new. They may say they don't have time for a new hobby or they already have enough friends. They procrastinate – that means they put off trying anything until another time, such as next week, or next term or even next year ... or they never get round to trying it at all!

Move on!

Some people will have a go at anything. If they fail they don't waste time blaming themselves or getting upset, they shrug and start thinking about what to do next. For others, failing at one thing can dent their self-confidence so much they don't believe they can do anything right.

Have a go!

Trying new things makes you feel more connected with life rather than just sitting on the sidelines watching everyone else. Want to try something new? Give it a go!

Try new things because...

⭐ If you don't try new things you'll never know if you could do them or not. Even if you're not perfect, you tried and that feels great.

⭐ Trying new things is fun. It stops you getting bored and makes you a more interesting person.

⭐ The more you try something new and enjoy it, the more you'll want to try new things. Win win!

Excuses, excuses! Have you ever used one of these excuses for not trying something different?

Who needs to know how to do that... it's such a waste of time.

That looks like fun but I'm too busy right now. Next time.

There's no point trying this as I know I won't be able to do it.

Not really my thing. I'll just stay here and watch.

HIGH EXPECTATIONS

Those who care about us want us to have good friends, a fulfilling job and a happy life. Our families and teachers want us to do well at school, and friends often need our support.

Climbing a mountain

There are lots of pressures on young people to do well at school, and to be popular, sporty, cool and grown up. Parents, teachers and friends all have their own expectations of us and it might seem that you have to please everyone else before you can please yourself. It can be like climbing a mountain.

Family expectations

Your family wants the best for you and for most this means a good education. It may seem that adults only care if you come first and that they don't appreciate all the hard work you do. If you fail an exam or test no one will think any less of you or love you less, and you shouldn't be too hard on yourself, either. It may be important for you to do well and to get good marks in certain subjects but there

Cultural expectations

In some cultures, academic success is very important. Parents expect their children to be top of the class or to get star plus grades and nothing less is acceptable. This can make a child feel that their parents won't love them if they don't come first, and that can make them obsessive about getting top grades. Try and talk to your parents about how their expectations are affecting you.

> *Success is the ability to go from failure to failure without losing your enthusiasm.*
>
> Winston Churchill
> (1874–1965),
> former UK Prime Minister

TALKBACK!

What do you think is the best attitude towards tests and exams?

You should do your best and see what happens. Take the good with the bad.

No point doing anything unless you can come first. Who wants to fail?

are always alternatives if things don't go exactly to plan. Talk to your teachers about how you can get your plans back on track if you fail an important exam.

If you have a real problem with a subject explain this to your teacher – maybe it's just not the right subject for you or there's a reason why you're having such difficulty with it. Don't be ashamed to ask for help – it's worse to struggle than to discuss the issues.

SCHOOL STRESS

Nearly everyone gets anxious about school and exams. But some students develop such a fear of 'getting it wrong' that it can seriously start to affect their health and how they feel.

Under pressure

Stress is when we think everyone expects too much from us and we just can't cope with it. For some people stress is a positive thing, it makes them feel excited and energised. For others it can have a very negative effect on their physical and mental health.

People with a fear of failure can feel really stressed and anxious when it comes to exams and tests, especially if they are under pressure from others to do well.

Stress test

Not eating or sleeping properly, stomach pains, headaches, feeling irritable, being snappy, depressed and feeling negative about everything are signs of stress. Stress is a vicious circle – the more anxious you feel, the more difficult it is to study and concentrate. This adds to your anxiety and you'll get more stressed. Feeling anxious before an exam is normal, but try not to let excessive stress affect your health by checking out the stress busters (see page 15).

Panic attacks!

Exam pressure can lead to panic attacks. This happens when extra adrenaline and other hormones start surging through your body. Symptoms include rapid breathing, feeling dizzy, sweating, breathlessness, thumping heartbeat, feeling sick, a ringing in your ears and chest pains or tightness. This can be scary but it's not dangerous. Take deep, slow breaths and try to calm yourself. The panic attack will pass. If these happen a lot, talk to a teacher, trusted adult or a friend or phone a helpline (see page 31).

Stress busters

Here are some ways to help you cope with stress:

- Don't snack on comfort foods like biscuits, crisps and chips. Try and eat regular meals and have lots of fruit and veggies. Drink water rather than fizzy drinks.

- Don't sit awake half the night revising. Make sure you get eight to ten hours' sleep a night.

- While revising take frequent breaks. Stand up, stretch, go for a walk, text a friend or read a bit of your favourite novel.

- Take regular exercise such as long walks, go swimming or take a cycle ride to clear your head and help you feel able to cope.

- Stay positive. Aim to do your best. It isn't the end of the world if you fail – you can usually take an exam or test again. Remember, many people fail but this doesn't stop them achieving great things (see pages 22-23).

Friends for ever?

We all want to have friends who like and respect us. But when friendships don't work out this is not a failure, it's just part of life's experiences.

Great mates

It's great to have a best friend we can talk to, laugh with and share our thoughts and secrets with. It's also great to be part of a group, a sports team or club or to have just a few mates to get together with. Interacting with others can really help our self-confidence and make us feel loved and part of something special.

Losing friends

Sometimes friends decide they want to be best friends with someone else or join a new crowd that you may not feel comfortable with. When a friendship ends it is sad and can make us feel lonely, but it's part of growing up and getting to know other people and ourselves. Unless we've done something deliberately to hurt or upset the other person, when a friendship ends it doesn't mean you aren't good or clever enough. People and situations change all the time.

LOVE

True friends

Some people think they are only liked because they are clever or funny or good at a sport or wear the latest fashions. They fear no one will like them for who they really are.

True friends will want to be with you because you are you and they feel comfortable in your company. They appreciate you for who you really are. With true friends you don't need to be afraid that they'll dump you or laugh if you don't get something right. Instead they will be there to sympathise when things go wrong and help you celebrate when things go right.

Amazing

Peer pressure

Some people can be so scared of losing their friends that they'll do things they don't want to do to keep in with them. This is called peer pressure. No one should feel they have to do something they don't want to because they might lose their friends or be bullied. Not doing something that you think is wrong or dangerous is not being a loser or a failure, it's being grown up and making up your own mind.

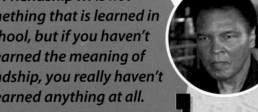

Friendship ... is not something that is learned in school, but if you haven't learned the meaning of friendship, you really haven't learned anything at all.

Muhammad Ali (1942 – 2016), champion boxer

#SMILE

Self-esteem and failure

Self-esteem is how we feel about ourselves – whether we think we're good or bad, a success or a failure. What we think about ourselves affects everything we do.

Good days, bad days

Some days we think we're great and can do anything we want to. Other days we can't seem to do anything right. Our levels of self-esteem are also influenced by how we think others see us, such as our family, friends and teachers. This may be affected by how well we do at sports or exams, or how popular we think we are.

Low and high self-esteem

Some people have low self-esteem most of the time. They say things like...

That's too hard for me.

I'm too slow to do that.

I'm not funny enough.

They focus on the things they've got wrong in the past, or couldn't do, rather than the things they did really well. On the other hand, people with high or healthy self-esteem are proud of what they achieve. They enjoy trying new things. If they fail, they may be disappointed or upset for a little while, but they soon put it behind them and move on to something new.

Friends and family

If we have supportive friends and family, we are more likely to have good, healthy self-esteem. If our family wants us to be the best all the time and friends criticise or mock us, this can lower our self-esteem. That's why it's good to have friends who are there for you whether you fail or succeed and who don't laugh or ridicule you if you fail. This works both ways; remember to be kind to friends who might be feeling bad about failing at something. Remind them that they are special to you, no matter what they succeed or fail at.

If a friend has done badly in a test in a subject they're not very good at, what is the best way to handle it?

Be honest. Tell them they're useless at the subject and to give up and stick to what they're best at.

Be supportive. At least they gave it a go. Not everyone is good at everything all the time.

MAKE FAILURE A SUCCESS

Failing might seem like the end of the world but it can be just another way of learning and growing. If you accept failure and learn from it, you can turn your failure into a success!

Failing helps you succeed

This may sound odd but think about it. When you fail at something you can learn from the mistakes you made. That means that if you try again, you probably won't make the same mistakes, so you have every chance of succeeding next time. The thing is not to be afraid of trying and failing ... and then trying again.

Failing gives you courage

When you fail you learn that the world doesn't fall apart and people still love you. Realising this is great and can give you the courage to have a go at other new things you'd like to try but were afraid to in case you failed!

Many people feel nervous about joining a new club or signing up for a new course, but be positive and think of it as a chance to make new friends and gain new skills or learn a new hobby. Trying something new gets easier each time you do it.

Failing gives you opportunities

If you've set your heart on doing something, such as learning the guitar, trying a new dive from the top board or being ace at art, not being as good as you want to be can be a big let-down and very disappointing. You might feel there's no point in bothering if you can't do what you really want. With supportive friends and family you'll get over it, and then you'll find you have the time to try something else. And maybe the new thing will be even better and more fun and that's a really exciting thought! The point is not to give up when you fail but to see it as an opportunity to try something different.

Failure in itself is not bad, it's what you learn from it and how you move on and grow from it that is important.

I'm useless at acting but really good at making costumes — I didn't even know I could sew.

Playing football wasn't for me but it's great going to the matches with my new mates.

My cakes always flop but I make a brilliant pizza.

I tried the violin but didn't really get on with it, so now I'm trying the drums and I'm not too bad.

Be inspired...

Many famous celebrities, medal winners and successful business gurus have faced failure but they just kept on trying and eventually they succeeded...

If I have a bad training session or haven't hit a time I wanted to hit, I feel gutted, but I never think, 'I've failed'.

Laura Trott (b. 1992–)
Olympic gold medal cyclist

Richard Branson (b. 1950–) has dyslexia and dropped out of school aged 15. But that didn't stop him from becoming one of the most successful businessmen in the world.

Bill Gates (b. 1955–) dropped out of university and failed at his first business. But he succeeded next time – creating the multimillion-dollar computer company Microsoft and becoming one of the richest men in the world!

Albert Einstein (1879–1955) is known as a modern-day genius, but he failed in his first attempt at the entrance exam to a polytechnic and had to try again. He went on to become one of the greatest and most well-known scientists of all time.

'It is impossible to live without failing at something, unless you live so cautiously that you might as well not have lived at all…'

J. K. Rowling (b. 1965–) author

Walt Disney (1901–66) was fired from his first job working for a newspaper because his boss thought he didn't have any 'good ideas'. Disney also failed in all his early business ventures. But he kept trying new things until he eventually found something he was good at…

WHAT IS *YOUR* SUCCESS?

Glamorous celebrities, a clever best friend, successful brother or sister... sometimes it's difficult to compete with all that success around us. But what does success mean to you?

Don't compare!

Just because your friend, or sister or cousin is really great at something doesn't mean that you have to be as well. Everyone has different skills and abilities and comparing yourself to others is pointless. Don't make yourself anxious by thinking about how much better everyone else is, but focus on your own strengths. There will be things that you are really good at that others aren't. Develop these strengths and enjoy the skills you have.

Your own success

What does success mean to you? Is it getting high marks at school? Being good at sport? Is it being popular and part of the cool group? Is your idea of success based on the media and what other people tell you is success, or your own goals and interests? Think about what you really want to succeed at, what makes you feel good about yourself and what you enjoy doing.

The 'halo effect'

Not many people are good at everything, but with some people it can seem that way due to the 'halo effect'. This is when we are dazzled by a person's success at one thing and believe they must be successful at everything they do. This also applies to how people look. Studies show that if a person is attractive we automatically believe they must be clever, kind and successful, but there is absolutely no reason for this to be true.

Role models

Role models are people whose values and achievements we admire and who we wish to be like, whether it's a sports person, author, actor or someone we know in school or locally who has done something brave or special. Role models should inspire us to be positive and show us that failure is an obstacle we can overcome.

Malala Yousafzai was shot by the Taliban for going to school.

For a friendship to really work, do you aways have to share the same interests and like the same things?

For me, being successful is fitting in with everyone else. What's the point of doing something that your friends can't do with you?

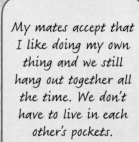

My mates accept that I like doing my own thing and we still hang out together all the time. We don't have to live in each other's pockets.

Overcoming your fear

There are lots of things you can do to help fight a fear of failure. The first is to know you're not alone ... lots of other people feel the same as you.

Be positive

You have to accept that you will fail at some things throughout your life and so will everybody else, and this is perfectly normal and acceptable. But if failing is a real issue for you, there are ways to help you cope:

- Think through what will happen if you fail. You and others may be disappointed, but you can be proud that you did your best. You can learn from the mistakes and try again, or move on to something else.

- Keep positive. Instead of worrying about all the things that can go wrong, imagine it all going right. Imagine how pleased you'll feel when you get the good exam results, or the cheers when you score a goal. See yourself receiving applause or praise and feeling proud of yourself.

- Write down a revision or work schedule for an exam or homework project. Having a plan will make you feel in control and give you a sense of achievement as you go through it.

You are not a failure

If you don't pass an exam or you're not in with the cool crowd this doesn't mean you're a failure as a person. The person you really are is based on things you can't see, such as how caring, kind and loving you are and how you treat others. We are not who we are because of our successes. Being successful doesn't automatically make you kind and fun to know!

Think about the people you love and who are close to you. Do you love them because they are successful or attractive or wear the latest styles? Or is it because they support you and understand you, make you laugh and give you hugs when you feel sad?

I've missed more than 9,000 shots in my career. I've lost almost 300 games. I've failed over and over and over again in my life. And that is why I succeed.

Michael Jordan (b. 1963–) the top US basketball player, failed to make his high school basketball team!

Try some positive thinking next time you're feeling anxious about failing.

I have done my best and I'm ready for the exam.

Whatever happens today, I am loved and loving.

I am confident, strong and will do my best.

People love me for who I am.

27

SO, TO RECAP...

These are some of the issues in this book, which are presented as ideas to discuss. Talking things through can help us to understand how we react to situations and how others feel. It also helps us to see that other people can feel the same way that we do.

Deal with your fear

Most people experience fear of failure at some time … they fear they might let someone down, disappoint a parent or teacher or feel stupid or embarrassed if they fail in front of their mates. What are some good ways to try and deal with this?

Unreal life

Every day we see images of glamorous, rich, successful celebrities. But is this what real life is like? Won't we fail if we try to be like them?

Try new things

No one is born with a fear of failure. This is something we pick up as we get older. Maybe we have only been praised for our successes and not for trying, and we've seen how disappointed people are if we fail. What do you think can happen if people become afraid to try new things because they think they will fail at them?

Make mistakes

Making mistakes can help us to grow and learn. They can teach us to cope with failure in a positive way by helping us to move on and try new things. What do you think are the best ways to look at failure so that it's a positive experience? Have you ever failed and had a positive outcome as a result?

Have a go

Failing can make some people extremely anxious and stop them from trying anything new. What would you say to a friend or brother or sister who felt like this? How would you persuade them to have a go even if they may not get it right? Does it matter if they fail? Isn't the trying more important?

Say no to the zone

People with a fear of failure can develop ways to stay safe in their comfort zone. They might procrastinate or say they don't want to try new stuff or they can't be bothered. How can you tell if someone is trying to hide a fear of failure? Have you used any excuses yourself to avoid trying something new? How can you get around this?

Glossary

academic to do with school and university and learning

adrenaline a hormone released by the adrenal gland when we feel stressed, anxious or get in a panic. Extra adrenaline in the body makes the heart beat faster and causes us to breathe faster.

anxiety feeling worried or nervous about how something is going to turn out; a feeling that things will not go well

ashamed feeling embarrassed or guilty at failing or not having done something well enough

cautiously carefully, safely

comfort zone a situation or familiar way of doing things or a place that you know well and that makes you feel safe

cope to be able to deal with something properly

cultures the beliefs and behaviour of different places and people

depressed feeling sad and negative and with no energy or enthusiasm for anything

expectations what people want you to achieve

goal something that you want to achieve

hormones chemical substances that travel around the body and help to keep it working properly

inadequate not good enough

lifestyle the way in which a person lives

low self-esteem feeling that you are not good enough, that you can't do things properly or well

obsessive thinking constantly about something

over-achiever someone who performs and achieves more and better than was expected

peer pressure when you feel you have to do something you don't want to because your friends or classmates are doing it

perspective keeping things in perspective, or in proportion, is a way of dealing with a situation calmly and realistically; not making it seem worse than it is

polytechnic a place of higher education at degree level

potential your abilities that can grow and become better and lead to success

pressure trying to influence someone to do something

procrastinate to keep putting off doing something; to make excuses not to do something until another time

ridicule to mock or make fun of someone

self-confidence the belief that you can achieve something or are good at doing things

self-esteem the way you feel about yourself and your abilities to achieve things

self-worth the belief that you should respect and value yourself and that you are worthy of the respect of others

stress worry; mental, physical or emotional strain

sympathise understand what someone is feeling

Taliban extreme Islamist military group

Learning new words helps you to express your feelings and to understand what you read in this book.

Further information

Note to parents and teachers: every effort has been made by the Publishers to ensure websites are suitable for children, that they are of the highest educational value, and that they contain no inappropriate or offensive material. However, because of the nature of the Internet, it is impossible to guarantee that the contents of these sites will not be altered. We strongly advise that Internet access is supervised by a responsible adult.

WEBSITES AND HELPLINES

If you feel overwhelmed by any of the issues you've read about in this book or need advice check out a website or call a helpline and talk to someone who will understand.

www.childline.org.uk

Find out about issues that are troubling you, meet others, message or call the 24 hour helpline for advice or someone who'll just listen.
Telephone: 0800 1111

www.huffingtonpost.com/lisabeth-saunders-medlock-phd/dont-fear-failure-9-powerful-lessons-we-can-learn-from-our-mistakes_b_6058380.html

Read about how we can use our mistakes to help us grow and succeed. It discusses owning our failures, accepting when we've failed, taking responsibility, learning from our mistakes and moving on.

http://personalexcellence.co/blog/overcome-fear-of-failure-student/

Understanding what a fear of failure is and positive ways to overcome it through three stages: Approval, Acceptance and Adventure.

https://successstory.com/inspiration/fear-of-failure

Aimed more at adults, but has some strong ideas about how you can overcome fear of failure and develop a positive approach to life.

www.youngminds.org.uk

Information and advice for children and young people experiencing bullying, stress and mental or emotional anxieties.

www.samaritans.org

A place where anyone can go for advice and comfort. The helpline is 08457 90 90 90.

www.sane.org/get-help

Online and phone help for mental and emotional issues with a dedicated helpline for young people.

www.supportline.org.uk

A charity giving emotional support to children and young people.

www.healthdirect.gov.au/partners/kids-helpline

A helpline for young people giving advice, counselling and support.

https://kidshelpline.com.au

Online and phone help for a wide range of issues.

www.kidsline.org.nz

Helpline run by specially trained young volunteers to help kids and teens deal with troubling issues and problems.

BOOKS

Be Positive! Think Positive! Feel Positive!
by Dr Orly Katz, Agam Publishing House, 2013
Advice on how to survive primary school by developing a positive attitude.

The Buzz
by David Hodgson, Crown House Publishing Ltd, 2009
A practical guide to how you can be your best. Find out what makes you buzz and then go for it!

Index

angry 8, 9
anxiety 4, 14, 29, 30

bullying 17

celebrities 7, 22–23, 24, 28
comfort zone 10, 29, 30
courage 20
criticism 6, 19

diet 15
disappointed 6, 9, 21

embarrassed 6, 8, 28
excuses 10, 11, 29
exercise 15
expectations 12, 13

family 7, 8, 12, 13, 18, 19, 21
friends 8, 9, 12, 16–17, 18, 19, 21

goals 9, 12, 25, 30

halo effect 24
hobbies 9, 10, 20
homework 5, 26

mistakes 6, 7, 8, 9, 20, 24, 26, 29

negative feelings 6, 8, 14

over-achieving 4, 30

panic attacks 15
peer pressure 17, 30
potential 10
praise 6, 12, 26
pressure 7, 12, 14
procrastinate 10, 29, 30
positive thinking 15, 21, 25, 26, 27, 29

revising 15
role models 25

sad 6, 18
school 4, 5, 9, 12, 14
self-confidence 4, 10, 11, 12, 16, 30
self-esteem 4, 18–19, 30
self-worth 4, 5, 30
sleeping 15
strengths 9
stress 5, 7, 14–15, 30
stress busters 15
success 5, 7, 8, 20–21, 24–25

teachers 7, 8, 12, 13, 18

weaknesses 9

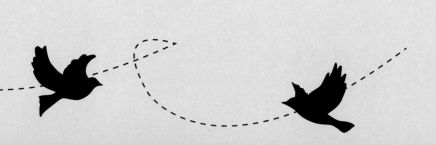

Fear of Failure

What is a fear of failure? • No one is born with a fear of failure • Making mistakes • Do you have a fear of failure? • High expectations • School stress • Friends for ever? • Self-esteem and failure • Make failure a success • Be inspired • What is *your* success? • Overcoming your fear

Cultural Issues

What is culture? • Culture and religion • Culture and law • A changing society • Stereotyping • Old v new • Clashes at home • Your rights matter • I am what I wear • Prejudice and discrimination • Dealing with prejudice • Respect!

Family Differences

A family today • Fighting families • Divorce • Single parent family • Trust and abuse • Manage your anger • Problems with siblings • Child carers • Living on the breadline • My life! • Family breakdown • Foster and adoption • Illness and death

Self-esteem and Confidence

What is self-esteem? • Body image • A healthy body image • You are unique • Being shy • What is self-confidence? • Pressure! • Being assertive • Learning difficulties • Bullied or bully?

Understanding Sexuality

Time for change • What is sexuality? • Being lesbian, gay or bisexual • Where do I fit in? • Setting the record straight • Coming out • Homophobia – it's not right • Dealing with bad feelings • Being accepted • Proud to be me!

Understanding Transgender

What is gender? • What is transgender? • Transgender is not LGB • The real me • Family support • School policy • Bullying and discrimination • Puberty – help! • Be inspired • Transitioning – the journey • Your true self